Ireland's Best Loved Songs and Ballads

For Easy Piano

CONTENTS

Order No. 11AWAL-1141
ISBN 978-1-85720-046-2

Exclusive Distributors: Waltons Publishing
Unit 6A, Rosemount Park Drive, Rosemount Business Park, Ballycoolin Road, Dublin 11, Ireland

waltons
publishing

A Bunch Of Thyme

G Bm   D7   G   C   G

no   man steal a - way your   thyme.

Chorus:—

For thyme it is a precious thing
And thyme brings all things to
    to my mind
Thyme, with all its flavours
Along with all its joys
Thyme, brings all things
    to my mind.

Once I had a bunch of thyme
I thought it never would decay
Then came a lusty sailor
Who chanced to pass my way
And stole my bunch of thyme
    away.

Repeat Chorus:—

The sailor gave to me a rose
A rose that never would decay
He gave it to me
To keep me reminded
Of when he stole my thyme
    away.

3

Carrickfergus

My childhood days bring back sad reflections of happy times I spent so long ago
My boyhood friends and my own relations have all passed on now like melting snow
But I'll spend my days in endless roaming, soft is the grass, my bed is free
Ah! to be back now in Carrickfergus, on that long road down to the sea.

And in Kilkenny, it is reported, there are marble stones as black as ink
With gold and silver I would support her, but I'll sing no more now till I get a drink
I'm drunk today, and I'm seldom sober, a handsome rover from town to town
Ah! but I'm sick now, my days are numbered, so come all ye young men and lay me down.

The Rose Of Tralee

Vale of Tra - lee. She was love - ly and fair as the Rose of the Sum - mer, yet 'twas not her beau - ty a - lone that won me. Oh no 'twas the truth in her eye ev - er dawn - ing that made me love

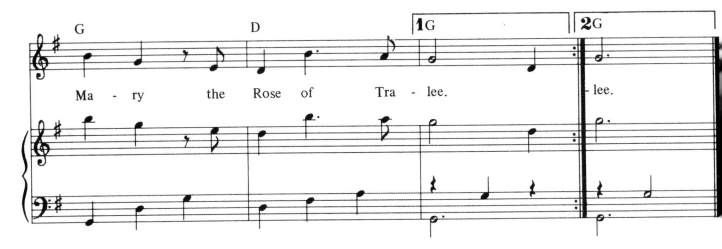

Ma - ry   the   Rose   of   Tra - lee.   - lee.

The cool shades of evening their mantles were spreading
And Mary, all smiling, sat listening to me
The moon thro' the valley her pale rays was shedding
When I won the heart of the Rose of Tralee.
Tho' lovely and fair as the rose of the summer
Yet, 'twas not her beauty alone that won me,
Oh! no, 'twas the truth in her eye ever dawning
That made me love Mary, the Rose of Tralee.

The Mall, Tralee, Co. Kerry.

The Sally Gardens

leaves grow up-on the tree. But I was young and
fool - ish and with her did not a - gree.

In a field down by the river my love and I did stand
And on my leaning shoulder, she laid her snow-white hand
She bid me take life easy, as the grass grows on the weirs
But I was young and foolish, and now am full of tears.

Down by the sally gardens, my love and I did meet
She passed the sally gardens, with little snow-white feet
She bid me take love easy, as the leaves grow on the tree
But I, being young and foolish, with her did not agree.

Danny Boy

And when ye come and all the flowers are dying
If I am dead, as dead I well may be
You'll come and find the place where I am lying
And kneel and say an Ave there for me.

Repeat Chorus: —

And I shall hear tho' soft you tread above me
And all my grave will warmer sweeter be
If you will bend and tell me that you love me
Then I shall sleep in peace until you come to me.

Ship Quay Place, Derry.

The Last Rose of Summer

blush - es an - d give _____ sigh for sigh I'll not

I'll not leave thee, thou lone one! to pine on the stem
Since the lovely are sleeping, go sleep thou with them
Thus kindly I scatter thy leaves o'er the bed
Where thy mates of the garden lie scentless and dead.

So soon may I follow, when friendships decay
And from love's shining circle the gems drop away
When true hearts lie wither'd and fond ones are flown
Oh! who would inhabit this bleak world alone!

Slievenamon

time and the joys that are gone, and I ne - ver will for-get the sweet

maid - en that I met in the val - ley of Slie - ve - na - mon.

It was not the grace of her queenly air; Nor her cheek of the rose's glow
Nor her soft black eyes, nor her flowing hair; Nor was it her lily white brow
'Twas the soul of truth and of melting ruth; And the smile like a summer dawn
That stole my heart away on a soft summer day; In the Valley near Slievenamon.

In the festive hall, by the starwashed shore; Ever my restless spirit cries
"My love, oh, my love, shall I ne'er see you more? And, my land, will you never uprise?"
By night, and by day, I ever, ever pray; While lonely my life flows on
To see our flag unfurled and my true-love to enfold; In the Valley near Slievenamon.

The Jug Of Punch

'Twas ve-ry ear-ly in the month of June As I was sit-ting with my glass and spoon. A small bird sat on an i-vy bush and the song he sang was the Jug of Punch. Toor-a loor-a-la, toor-a loor-a-lae, toor-a-loor-a-la, toor-a

-loor - a - lae._____ A small bird sat on an

iv - y bush and the song he sang was the Jug of Punch.

If I were sick and very bad, and was not able to go or stand
I would not think it at all amiss to pledge my shoes for a jug of punch.

Repeat Chorus:—

What more divarsion can a man desire than to sit him down by a snug turf fire
Upon his knee a pretty wench, and upon his table a jug of punch.

Repeat Chorus.—

And when I'm dead and in my grave, no costly tombstone will I have
I'll dig a grave both wide and deep, with a jug of punch at my head and feet.

Repeat Chorus:—

Arcade. New Tipperary.

19

Cockles And Mussels

She was a fishmonger; But sure 'twas no wonder
For so were her father and mother before; And they both wheeled their barrow
Through streets broad and narrow; Crying cockles and mussels, alive, alive, oh!

Repeat Chorus:—

She died of a fever; And no one could save her
And that was the end of sweet Molly Malone; But her ghost wheels her barrow
Through street broad and narrow; Crying cockles and mussels, alive, alive, oh!

Repeat Chorus:—

I'll Take You Home Again Kathleen

I'll take you home a-gain Kath-leen, A - cross the o-cean wild and wide. To where your heart has e - ver been, Since first you were my bon - ny bride. The ros - es all have left your cheeks ___ I've

green _____ I'll take you to your home Kath-leen.

I know you love me, Kathleen dear, your heart was ever fond and true
I always fear when you are near, that life holds nothing dear but you
The smiles that once you gave to me, I scarcely ever see them now
Though many, many times I see, a dark'ning shadow on your brow.

Repeat Chorus:—

To that dear home beyond the sea. my Kathleen shall again return
And when thy old friends welcome thee, thy loving heart will cease to yearn
Where laughs the little silver stream, beside your mother's humble cot
And brighter rays of sunshine gleam, there all your grief will be forgot

Repeat Chorus:—

An Irish Village

24

Spancil Hill

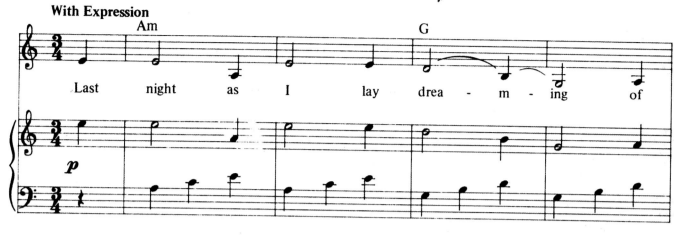

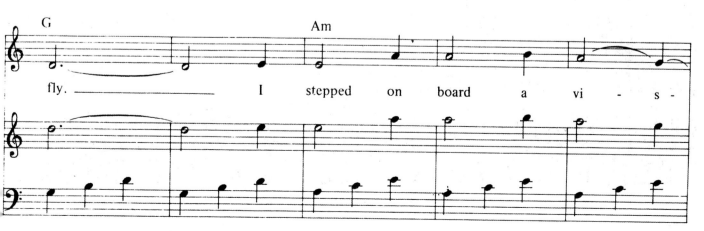

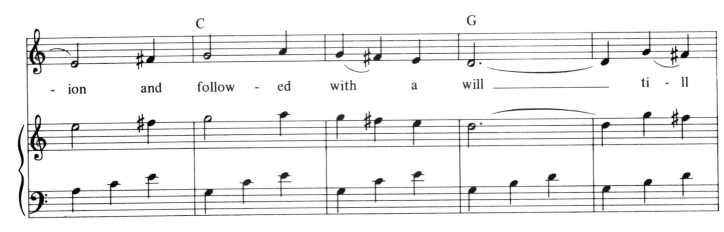

-ion and follow -ed with a will _____ ti -ll

next I came to an - chor at the

cross near Span - cil Hill. _____

Delighted by the novelty, enchanted with the scene
Where in my early boyhood where often I had been
I thought I heard a murmer and I think I hear it still
It's the little stream of water that flows down Spancil Hill.

To amuse a passing fancy I lay down on the ground
And all my school companions they shortly gathered round
When we were home returning we danced with bright goodwill
To Martin Moynahan's music at the cross at Spancil Hill.

It was on the twenty-fourth of June the day before the fair
When Ireland's sons and daughters and friends assembled there
The young, the old, the brave and the bold came their duty to fulfill.
At the parish church in Clooney, a mile from Spancil Hill.

I went to see my neighbours to see what they might say
The old ones they were dead and gone, the young ones turning grey
I met the tailor Quigley, he as bold as ever still
For he used to make my britches when I lived at Spancil Hill.

I paid a flying visit to my first and only love
She's as fair as any lily and gentle as a dove
She threw her arms around me, crying Johnny I love you still
She was a farmer's daughter, the pride of Spancil Hill.

Well I dreamt I hugged and kissed her as in the days of yore
She said, Johnny you're only joking as many the time before
The cock crew in the morning, he crew both loud and shrill
And I woke in California, many miles from Spancil Hill.

The Spinning Wheel

Mel - low   the moon-light to shine is   be - gin - ning.

Close by   the win - dow young Eil - een is   spin - ning.   Bent o'er the fire   her blind

Grand-mo-ther sit - ting,   is   croon-ing and moan - ing and   drow - si - ly knit - ting.

Mer - ri-ly,   cheer - i - ly,   nois - i - ly whir - ring.   Swings the wheel spins the wheel

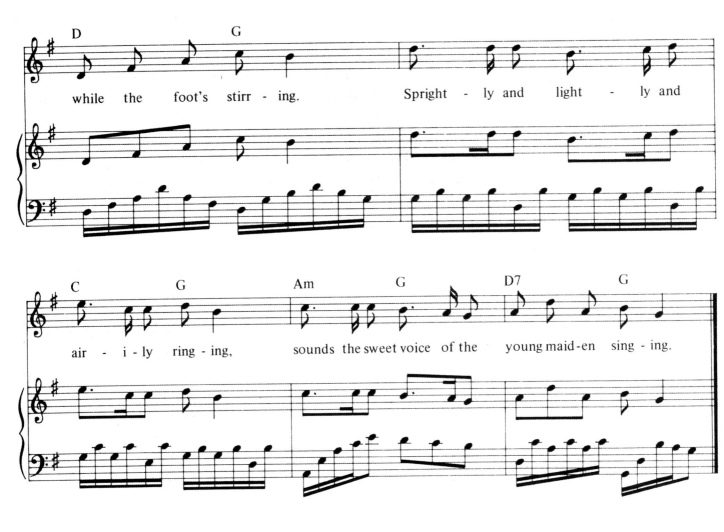

while the foot's stirr - ing. Spright - ly and light - ly and

air - i - ly ring - ing, sounds the sweet voice of the young maid-en sing - ing.

Eileen, a chara, I hear someone tapping
'Tis the ivy dear mother against the glass flapping
Eily, I surely hear somebody sighing
'Tis the sound mother dear of the autumn winds dying.

What's the noise that I hear at the window I wonder?
'Tis the little birds chirping, the holly-bush under
What makes you be shoving and moving your stool on?
And singing all wrong the old song of 'The Coolin'?

There's a form at the casement, the form of her true love
And he whispers with face bent, I'm waiting for you, love
Get up on the stool, through the lattice step lightly
And we'll rove in the grove while the moon's shining brightly.

The maid shakes her head, on her lips lays her fingers
Steps up from the stool, longs to go and yet lingers
A frightened glance turns to her drowsy grandmother
Puts one foot on the stool, spins the wheel with the other.

Lazily, easily, swings now the wheel round
Slowly and lowly is heard now the reel's sound
Noiseless and light to the lattice above her
The maid steps, then leaps to the arms of her lover.

Slower and slower and slower the wheel rings
Lower and lower and lower the reel rings
E're the reel and the wheel stop their ringing and moving
Through the grove the young lovers by moonlight are roving.

The Spinning Wheel

Matt Hyland

There was a lord, who lived in the
town, who had a love-ly hand-some daugh-ter.
She was court-ed by a fair young man
who was a ser-vant to her fath-er. But

So straight away to her love she goes, into his room to awake him
Saying "arise my love and go away, this very night you will be taken.
I over-heard my parents say, in spite of me they will transport you
So arise my love and go away, I wish to God I'd gone before you".

They both sat down upon the bed, just for the side of one half hour
And not a word by either said, as down their cheecks the tears did shower
She laid her hand upon his breast, around his neck her arms entwined
Not a duke nor lord nor an earl I'll wed, I'll wait for you my own Matt Hyland.

The lord discoursed with his daughter fair, one night alone in her chamber
Saying "we'll give you leave for to bring him back, Since there's no one can win your favour
She wrote a letter then in haste, her heart for him was still repining
They brought him back, to the church they went and made a lord of young Matt Hyland.

The Black Velvet Band

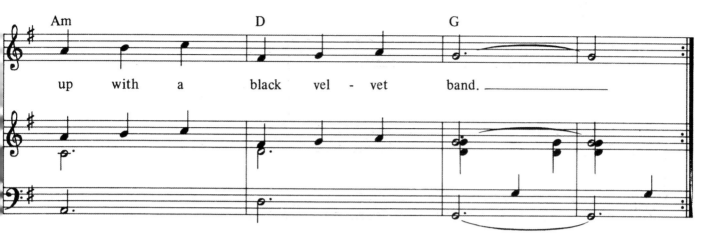

up with a black vel - vet band. _____

As I went walking down Broadway; Not intending to stay very long
I met with a frolicksome damsel, As she came tripping along.

A watch she pulled out of her pocket, And slipped it right into my hand
On the very first day that I met her, Bad luck to the black velvet band.

Before judge and jury next morning, Both of us did appear
A gentleman claimed his jewellery, And the case against us was clear.

Seven long years transportation, Right down to "Van Dieman's Land"
Faw away from my friends and companions, Betrayed by the black velvet band.

Irish Jaunting Car

The Mountains Of Mourne

Oh Ma - ry this Lon - don's a won - der - ful sight with peo - ple here work - ing by day and by night. They don't sow po - ta - toes nor bar - ley nor wheat but there's

gangs of them dig - ging for gold on the

streets. At least when I asked them that's

what I was told, So I just took a

hand at this dig - ging for gold. But for

I believe that when writin' a wish you expressed
As to how the fine ladies in London were dressed
Well if you believe me, when asked to a ball
Faith they don't wear a top to their dresses at all
Oh, I've seen them myself and you could not in truth
Say if they were bound for a ball or a bath,
Don't be startin' them fashions now, Mary macree
Where the Mountains of Mourne sweep down to the sea.

I've seen England's king from the top of a bus
I've never known him, tho' he means to know us
And tho' by the Saxon we once were oppressed
Still I cheered, God forgive me, I cheered with the rest
And now that he's visited Erin's green shore
We'll be much better friends than we've been heretofore
When we've got all we want we're as quiet as can be
Where the Mountains of Mourne sweep down to the sea.

You remember young Peter O'Loughlin of course
Well now he is here at the head of the Force
I met him today, I was crossing the Strand
And he stopped the whole street with one wave of his hand
And there we stood talkin' of days that are gone
While the whole population of London looked on
But for all these great powers he's wishful, like me
To be back where the dark Mourne sweeps down to the sea.

There's beautiful girls here—oh never you mind
With beautiful shapes Nature never designed
And lovely complexions all roses and cream
But O'Loughlin remarked with regard to the same
That if at those roses you venture to sip
The colours might all come away on your lip
So I'll wait for the wild rose that's waitin' for me
Where the Mountains of Mourne sweep down to the sea.

The Lark In The Clear Air

Dear_ thoughts are in_ my_ mind_ and my_ soul soars_ en-chant-ed as I hear the sweet_ lark_ sing_ in the_ clear_ air of the day. For a ten-der beam-ing_ smile to my

ho - pe has been grant - ed and to - mor - row she shall

hear all my fond heart wou - ld say.

I shall tell her all my love, all my soul's adoration
And I think she will hear me, and will not say me nay.
It is this that gives my soul all its joyous elation
As I hear the sweet lark sing in the clear air of the day.

Avoca, Co. Wicklow.

The Old Woman From Wexford

Oh there was an old wo-man from Wex-ford and in Wex-ford she did dwell. _____ She loved her old man dear-ly but an-oth-er one as well, _____ with your rum dum dum dum dei-ro and the

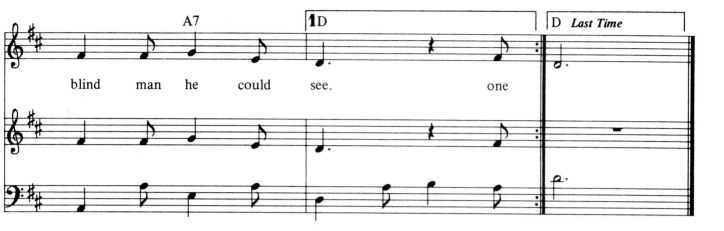

blind   man   he   could   see.   one

One day she went to the doctor,
some medicine for to find.
She said 'will you give me something
for to make me old man blind'.

'Feed him eggs and marrowbones
and make him suck them all,
And it won't be very long after
till he won't see you at all'.

The doctor wrote a letter
and he signed it with his hand.
He sent it round to the old man,
just to let him understand.

She fed him eggs and marrowbones
and made him suck them all,
And it wasn't very long after till
he couldn't see the wall.

Says he: 'I'd like to drown myself,
but that might be a sin',
Says she: 'I'll go along with you
and help to push you in'.

The woman she stepped back a bit
for to rush and push him in,
And the old man quickly stepped aside
and she went tumblin'in.

Oh how loudly she did yell
and how loudly she did call.
'Yerra hold your whist old woman,
sure I can't see you at all'.

Now eggs and eggs and marrowbones
may make your old man blind,
But if you want to drown him,
you must creep up close behind.

The Rising Of The Moon

"Oh then, tell me Sean O'Farrell, where the gath'rin is to be?
In the old spot by the river well known to you and me
One word more for signal token, whistle up the marchin' tune,
With your pike upon your shoulder, by the risin' of the moon".

Out from many a mud wall cabin eyes were watching through that night
Many a manly heart was throbbing for the blessed warning light
Murmurs passed along the valleys, like the banshee's lonely croon
And a thousand blades were flashing at the risin' of the moon.

There beside the singing river, that dark mass of men were seen
Far above the shining weapons hung their own beloved green
"Death to every foe and traitor! Forward! strike the marching tune
And hurrah, my boys, for freedom, 'tis the risin' of the moon".

Well they fought for poor old Ireland, and full bitter was their fate
(O, what glorious pride and sorrow fills the name of Ninety-Eight!)
Yet, thank God, e'en still are beating hearts in manhood's burning noon,
Who would follow in their footsteps at the risin' of the moon!

The Connemara Cradle Song

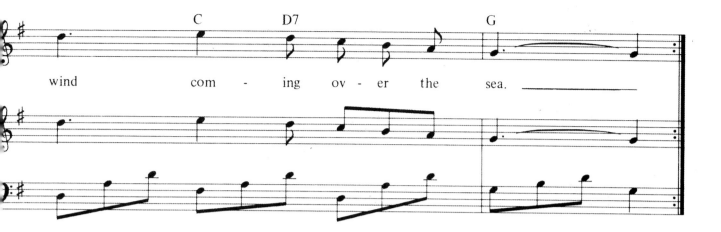

wind   com -   ing   ov - er   the   sea.

Chorus:—

Hear the wind blow love, hear the wind blow
Lean your head over and hear the wind blow

(Repeat)

The currachs are sailing way out on the blue
Chasing the herring of silvery hue
Silver the herring and silver the sea
Soon they'll be silver for baby and me.

Repeat Chorus:—

Oh winds of the night may your fury be crossed
May no one that's dear to our island be lost
Blow the wind gently calm be the foam
Shine the light brightly to guide them home.

Repeat Chorus:—

The curraghs tomorrow will stand on the shore
And Daddy goes sailing a sailing no more
The nets will be drying the nets heaven blessed
And safe in my arms dear contented he'll rest.

Repeat Chorus:—

The Claddagh, Co. Galway.

The Wild Rover

I went to an ale-house I used to frequent
And I told the landlady my money was spent
I asked her for credit, she answered me 'nay
Such a custom like yours I could have any day'.

Repeat Chorus:—

I took from my pocket ten sovereigns bright
And the landlady's eyes opened wide with delight
She said 'I have whiskey and wines of the best
And the words that I spoke sure were only in jest'.

Repeat Chorus:—

I'll go home to my parents, confess what I've done
And I'll ask them to pardon their prodigal son
And if they caress me as oft times before
Sure I never will play the wild rover no more.

Repeat Chorus:—